DAREDEVIL
SPORTS

ICE CLIMBING

By Hal Garrison

 Gareth Stevens
PUBLISHING

HOT
TOPICS

Please visit our website, www.garethstevens.com. For a free color catalog of all our high-quality books, call toll free 1-800-542-2595 or fax 1-877-542-2596.

Cataloging-in-Publication Data

Names: Garrison, Hal.
Title: Ice climbing / Hal Garrison.
Description: New York : Gareth Stevens Publishing, 2018. | Series: Daredevil sports | Includes index.
Identifiers: LCCN ISBN 9781538211175 (pbk.) | ISBN 9781538211199 (library bound) | ISBN 9781538211182 (6 pack)
Subjects: LCSH: Snow and ice climbing--Juvenile literature. | Extreme sports--Juvenile literature.
Classification: LCC GV200.3 B35 2018 | DDC 796.9--dc23

Published in 2018 by
Gareth Stevens Publishing
111 East 14th Street, Suite 349
New York, NY 10003

Designer: Bethany Perl
Editor: Kate Mikoley

Photo credits: Cover, pp. 1, 10 Vitalii Nesterchuk/Shutterstock.com; pp. 1-32 (background) Cyrustr/Shutterstock.com; p. 5 Tomas Laburda/Shutterstock.com; p. 6 Victorstock/Shutterstock.com; p. 7 anse/Shutterstock.com; pp. 8, 13 My Good Images/Shutterstock.com; p. 9 Simon Dannhauer/Shutterstock.com; p. 11 Lone Pine/Shutterstock.com; p. 15 aragami12345s/Shutterstock.com; p. 17 Rubanov Vladimir/Shutterstock.com; p. 18 Qu3a/Wikipedia.org; p. 19 Federico Rostagno/Shuttersock.com; p. 21 Pecold/Shutterstock.com; p. 23 Marko5/Shutterstock.com; p. 25 MFlynn/Shutterstock.com; p. 27 Don Mason/Blend Images/Getty Images; p. 29 Sergei Kazantsev/Wikipedia.org.

Printed in the United States of America

CPSIA compliance information: Batch #CW18GS: For further information contact Gareth Stevens, New York, New York at 1-800-542-2595.

CONTENTS

WHAT'S ICE CLIMBING?

Imagine climbing a very steep mountain, but the sides are covered with ice. Every move must be a careful one. One wrong step, and the climb could be over. The view is beautiful at the top, but it takes a daredevil to get there!

RISK FACTOR

Ice climbing is the act of climbing up steep, often vertical, frozen water or snow.

The first ice climbers were likely rock climbers. Many tall mountains and rock walls get icy near the top. Climbers came up with ways to make their way past these tricky spots. Some liked it so much they started looking for completely frozen places to climb.

ROCK CLIMBER

RISK FACTOR

Ice climbers often seek out tall ice forms such as glaciers and frozen waterfalls.

KINDS OF ICE

There are two main kinds of ice people climb. High up in the mountains, there's often a lot of snow. As time passes, the snow can become packed together and hard. This is called alpine ice.

RISK FACTOR

Mountain glaciers are alpine ice. They can be very steep, but are usually not totally vertical.

The second type of ice is water ice. This is simply frozen water, such as a waterfall. This kind of climbing is often completely vertical. Water ice can sometimes form many **icicles**, which can break off and fall.

RISK FACTOR

All ice climbers need to be well trained. Many take special classes before attempting to climb a waterfall or icy mountain.

GET IN GEAR

Ice climbing can be much like rock climbing. Both kinds of climbing require special equipment, or gear. However, since ice climbers are commonly climbing in much trickier and colder conditions, they need equipment specially made for their sport.

RISK FACTOR

Even skilled ice climbers wear helmets to keep safe from falling bits of ice.

HELMET

13

GET A GRIP!

Ice climbers need to be able to get a good grip, or hold, on the ice. That's why ice climbers use one or two axes. The sharp part, called the pick, goes into the ice. While holding the ax, climbers use their legs to push up.

RISK FACTOR

Many ice-climbing tools have leashes, or ropes that connect the tool to the climber so they don't drop it.

AXES

PICK

LEASH

15

Another way ice climbers grip the ice is with crampons. These are tools that go on the bottom of the boot or shoe. They have sharp points that dig into the ice so the climber's foot doesn't slip.

RISK FACTOR

Before crampons were invented, ice climbers had to cut steps into the ice for their feet!

CRAMPONS

CLIPPING IN

Like rock climbers, some ice climbers use special ropes and tools to keep them from falling. This is called belaying. Ice climbers place screws in the ice and clip them to their rope. This way, if they slip, they won't fall to the ground.

SCREW

ROPE

SCREW

RISK FACTOR

Ice screws are only as strong as the ice they're in. Climbers look for the most **stable** parts of the ice to put their screws in.

DON'T BREAK THE ICE!

Some ice can break easily. This is called brittle ice. If the temperature gets hot, ice can also melt quickly. Brittle and melting ice can make climbing unsafe. Skilled climbers know how to spot trouble areas in ice.

RISK FACTOR

"Dinner plating" is when pieces, or plates, of brittle ice break off as a climber tries to hit their pick into it.

A CHILLY CLIMB

Water generally turns to ice at 32°F (0°C), so colder temperatures might seem better for ice climbing. However, extremely cold ice can break easily. Many ice climbers say the best temperature for climbing is between 14°F (-10°C) and 30°F (-1°C).

RISK FACTOR

When temperatures drop, strong climbing ice can sometimes form in just 2 days.

23

Shivering cold temperatures could bring other problems, too. If the temperature in a person's body gets too low, it could be very harmful. Ice climbers make sure to wear cold-weather gear to keep warm and safe on their climbs.

RISK FACTOR

Many climbers carry a first aid kit with them to treat **injuries**, such as **frostbite**.

CLIMBING INSIDE

Like any other sport, people who ice climb need lots of practice. Many start learning basic climbing skills by going to indoor rock-climbing gyms. Some places even have special climbing walls that make it seem like you're climbing ice.

RISK FACTOR

In Scotland, there's an indoor ice-climbing wall that uses up to 550 tons (500 mt) of real ice and snow!

A GROWING SPORT

The first known ice-climbing **competition** took place more than 100 years ago! Today, ice-climbing events are held all over the world. Some people even hope that the sport will someday become an event in the Winter Olympics!

RISK FACTOR

Though it wasn't included in the official games, ice climbing was **demonstrated** at the Olympic Park during the 2014 Winter Games in Sochi, Russia.

02:12:82

03:42:18

29

SAFETY TIPS

ALL ICE CLIMBERS SHOULD

- have proper climbing gear and know how to use it correctly.

- be able to tell if ice is stable or might break.

- wear a helmet and clothing suitable for cold weather.

- climb with a buddy or a group.

- carry and know how to use the tools in a first aid kit.

- stay in good shape by taking classes or practicing on rock walls.

FOR MORE INFORMATION

BOOKS

Butler, Erin K. *Extreme Snow and Ice Sports*. North Mankato, MN: Capstone Press, 2018.

Young, Jeff C. *Belaying the Line: Mountain, Rock, and Ice Climbing*. Edina, MN: ABDO Publishing, 2011.

WEBSITES

Ice Climbing
www.nationalgeographic.org/media/ice-climbing/
Watch a video about two climbers' adventure to the top of a frozen waterfall here.

Ice Climbing 101
www.kidzworld.com/article/7598-ice-climbing-101
Read more about the basics of the exciting yet dangerous sport of ice climbing on this site.

GLOSSARY

competition: an event in which people try to win

demonstrate: to show something, such as a skill, to other people

frostbite: a condition in which part of your body freezes or almost freezes

icicle: a hanging piece of ice formed when water freezes as it drips down from something

injury: a hurt, harm, or wound

stable: not easily moved

INDEX